family favourites
chocolate

Bath · New York · Singapore · Hong Kong · Cologne · Delhi · Melbourne

boston crème pie

ingredients

SERVES 6

225 g/8 oz ready-made
    shortcrust pastry

filling

3 eggs

115 g/4 oz caster sugar

150 g/5 oz plain flour, plus
    extra for dusting

1 tbsp icing sugar

pinch of salt

1 tsp vanilla essence

400 ml/14 fl oz milk

150 ml/5 fl oz plain yogurt

150 g/5$1/2$ oz plain chocolate,
    broken into pieces

2 tbsp Kirsch

to decorate

150 ml/5 fl oz sour cream

225 g/8 oz plain chocolate
    shavings or caraque

method

1 Roll out the pastry and use to line a 23-cm/ 9-inch loose-based tart tin. Prick the base with a fork, line with baking parchment, and fill with baking beans. Bake in a preheated oven, 200°C/400°F, for 20 minutes. Remove the beans and paper and return the pastry case to the oven for a further 5 minutes. Remove from the oven and place on a wire rack to cool.

2 To make the filling, beat the eggs and caster sugar in a heatproof bowl until fluffy. Sift in the flour, icing sugar and salt. Stir in the vanilla essence.

3 Bring the milk and yogurt to the boil in a small saucepan and strain it over the egg mixture. Set the bowl over a saucepan of barely simmering water. Stir the custard until it coats the back of a spoon.

4 Gently heat the chocolate with the Kirsch in a separate small saucepan until the chocolate has melted. Stir into the custard. Remove from the heat and stand the bowl in cold water. Set aside to cool.

5 Pour the chocolate mixture into the pastry case. Spread the sour cream evenly over the chocolate and decorate with chocolate shavings or caraque.

chocolate meringue pie

ingredients

SERVES 6

225 g/8 oz plain chocolate
    digestive biscuits
4 tbsp butter

filling

3 egg yolks
4 tbsp caster sugar
4 tbsp cornflour
600 ml/1pint milk
100 g/3^1/$_2$ oz plain chocolate,
    melted

meringue

2 egg whites
100 g/3^1/$_2$ oz caster sugar
^{1}/$_4$ tsp vanilla essence

method

1 Place the chocolate digestives in a plastic bag and crush with a rolling pin, then transfer to a large bowl. Place the butter in a small, heavy-based saucepan and heat gently until just melted, then stir it into the biscuit crumbs until well mixed. Press into the bottom and up the sides of a 23-cm/9-inch tart tin or dish.

2 To make the filling, place the egg yolks, caster sugar and cornflour in a large bowl and beat until they form a smooth paste, adding a little of the milk, if necessary. Place the milk in a small, heavy-based saucepan and heat gently until almost boiling, then slowly pour it onto the egg mixture, whisking well.

3 Return the mixture to the pan and cook gently, whisking, until thick. Remove from the heat. Whisk in the melted chocolate, then pour it onto the biscuit base.

4 To make the meringue, whisk the egg whites in a large, spotlessly clean, greasefree bowl until soft peaks form. Gradually whisk in two-thirds of the sugar until the mixture is stiff and glossy. Fold in the remaining sugar and vanilla essence.

5 Spread the meringue over the filling, swirling the surface with the back of a spoon to give it an attractive finish. Bake in the centre of a preheated oven, 160°C/375°F, for 30 minutes, or until golden. Serve hot or just warm.

pecan & chocolate pie

ingredients

SERVES 6–8

pastry

175 g/6 oz plain flour, plus
  extra for dusting
100 g/3^{1}/$_{2}$ oz butter, diced
1 tbsp golden caster sugar
1 egg yolk, beaten with
  1 tbsp water

filling

55 g/2 oz butter
3 tbsp cocoa powder
225 ml/8 fl oz golden syrup
3 eggs
70 g/2^{1}/$_{2}$ oz firmly packed
  dark brown sugar
175 g/6 oz shelled pecan
  nuts, chopped

to serve

whipped cream
ground cinnamon,
  for dusting

method

1 To make the pastry, sift the flour into a large bowl. Rub in the butter until the mixture resembles fine breadcrumbs, then stir in the caster sugar. Stir in the beaten egg yolk. Knead lightly to form a firm dough, cover with clingfilm and chill in the refrigerator for 1^{1}/$_{2}$ hours. Roll out the chilled pastry on a lightly floured work surface and use it to line a 20-cm/ 8-inch tart tin.

2 To make the filling, place the butter in a small, heavy-based saucepan and heat gently until melted. Sift in the cocoa and stir in the syrup. Place the eggs and sugar in a large bowl and beat together. Add the syrup mixture and the chopped pecan nuts and stir. Pour the mixture into the prepared pastry case.

3 Place the pie on a preheated baking sheet and bake in a preheated oven, 190°C/375°F, for 35–40 minutes, or until the filling is just set. Leave it to cool slightly and serve warm with a spoonful of whipped cream, dusted with ground cinnamon.

mississippi mud pie

ingredients

SERVES 8

pastry

225 g/8 oz plain flour, plus
    extra for dusting

2 tbsp cocoa powder

150 g/5$\frac{1}{2}$ oz butter

2 tbsp caster sugar

1–2 tbsp cold water

filling

175 g/6 oz butter

350 g/12 oz brown sugar

4 eggs, lightly beaten

4 tbsp cocoa powder, sifted

150 g/5$\frac{1}{2}$ oz plain chocolate

300 ml/10 fl oz single cream

1 tsp chocolate extract

to decorate

425 ml/15 fl oz double
    cream, whipped

chocolate flakes and curls

method

1 To make the pastry, sift the flour and cocoa into a mixing bowl. Rub in the butter with the fingertips until the mixture resembles fine breadcrumbs. Stir in the sugar and enough cold water to mix to a soft dough. Wrap the dough and chill in the refrigerator for 15 minutes.

2 Roll out the pastry on a lightly floured work surface and use to line a 23-cm/9-inch loose-based tart tin or ceramic pie dish. Line with baking parchment and fill with baking beans. Bake in a preheated oven, 190°C/375°F, for 15 minutes. Remove from the oven and take out the beans and parchment. Bake the pastry case for a further 10 minutes.

3 To make the filling, beat the butter and sugar together in a bowl and gradually beat in the eggs with the cocoa. Melt the chocolate and beat it into the mixture with the single cream and the chocolate extract.

4 Reduce the oven temperature to 160°C/325°F. Pour the mixture into the pastry case and bake for 45 minutes, or until the filling has set gently.

5 Allow the mud pie to cool completely, then transfer it to a serving plate, if you like. Cover with the whipped cream. Decorate the pie with chocolate flakes and curls and then chill until ready to serve.

chocolate crumble pie

ingredients

SERVES 8

pastry

200 g/7 oz plain flour

1 tsp baking powder

115 g/4 oz unsalted butter,
    cut into small pieces

25 g/1 oz caster sugar

1 egg yolk

1–2 tsp cold water

filling

150 ml/5 fl oz double cream

150 ml/5 fl oz milk

225 g/8 oz plain chocolate,
    chopped

2 eggs

crumble topping

100 g/3^1/$_2$ oz brown sugar

85 g/3 oz toasted pecan nuts

115 g/4 oz plain chocolate

85 g/3 oz amaretti biscuits

1 tsp cocoa powder

method

1 To make the pastry, sift the flour and baking powder into a large bowl, rub in the butter, and stir in the sugar, then add the egg and a little water to bring the pastry together. Turn the pastry out and knead briefly. Wrap the pastry and chill in the refrigerator for 30 minutes.

2 Preheat the oven to 190°C/375°F. Roll out the pastry and use to line a 23-cm/9-inch loose-based tart tin. Prick the pastry case with a fork. Line with baking parchment and fill with baking beans. Bake in the oven for 15 minutes. Remove from the oven and take out the beans and parchment. Reduce the oven temperature to 180°C/350°F.

3 Bring the cream and milk to the boil in a saucepan, remove from the heat, and add the chocolate. Stir until melted and smooth. Beat the eggs and add to the chocolate mixture, mix thoroughly and pour into the shell. Bake for 15 minutes, remove from the oven and leave it to rest for 1 hour.

4 When you are ready to serve the pie, place the topping ingredients in a food processor and pulse to chop. (If you do not have a processor, place the sugar in a large bowl, chop the nuts and chocolate with a large knife, and crush the biscuits, then add to the bowl with the cocoa and mix well.) Sprinkle over the pie, then serve it in slices.

hot chocolate cheesecake

ingredients

SERVES 8

butter, for greasing

pastry

150 g/5$\frac{1}{2}$ oz plain flour

2 tbsp cocoa powder

75 g/2$\frac{3}{4}$ oz butter, diced

2 tbsp golden caster sugar

25 g/1 oz ground almonds

1 egg yolk

icing sugar, for dusting

filling

2 eggs, separated

75 g/2$\frac{3}{4}$ oz golden caster
    sugar

350 g/12 oz cream cheese

40 g/1$\frac{1}{2}$ oz ground almonds

150 ml/5 fl oz double cream

25 g/1 oz cocoa powder,
    sifted

1 tsp vanilla essence

method

1 To make the pastry, sift the flour and cocoa powder into a bowl. Add the butter and rub it in until the mixture resembles fine breadcrumbs. Stir in the sugar and almonds. Add the egg yolk and enough water to make a soft dough. Roll out on a lightly floured work surface and use to line a 20-cm/8-inch loose-based cake tin greased with butter. Chill in the refrigerator while preparing the filling.

2 To make the filling, place the egg yolks and caster sugar in a large bowl and whisk together until thick and pale. Whisk in the cheese, almonds, cream, cocoa and vanilla essence until blended.

3 Place the egg whites in a clean, greasefree bowl and whisk until stiff but not dry. Stir a little of the whisked egg whites into the cheese mixture, then fold in the remainder. Pour into the pastry case. Bake in a preheated oven, 160°C/325°F, for 1$\frac{1}{2}$ hours, or until risen and just firm to the touch. Remove from the tin and dust with icing sugar.

chocolate bread pudding

ingredients

SERVES 4

6 thick slices white bread,
   crusts removed
450 ml/16 fl oz milk
175 ml/6 fl oz canned
   evaporated milk
2 tbsp cocoa powder
2 eggs
2 tbsp brown sugar
1 tsp vanilla essence
icing sugar,
   for dusting

hot fudge sauce

55 g/2 oz plain chocolate,
   broken into pieces
1 tbsp cocoa powder
2 tbsp golden syrup
55 g/2 oz butter or margarine
2 tbsp brown sugar
150 ml/5 fl oz milk
1 tbsp cornflour

method

1 Grease a shallow ovenproof dish. Cut the bread into squares and layer them in the dish.

2 Put the milk, evaporated milk and cocoa powder in a saucepan and heat gently, stirring occasionally, until the mixture is lukewarm. Whisk the eggs, sugar and vanilla essence together. Add the warm milk mixture and beat well.

3 Pour into the prepared dish, making sure that all the bread is completely covered. Cover the dish with clingfilm and chill in the refrigerator for 1–2 hours, then bake in a preheated oven 180°C/350°F, for 35–40 minutes, until set. Stand for 5 minutes.

4 To make the sauce, put all the ingredients into a saucepan and heat gently, stirring constantly until smooth.

5 Dust the chocolate bread pudding with icing sugar and serve immediately with the hot fudge sauce.

rich chocolate ice cream

ingredients

SERVES 6

ice cream

1 egg

3 egg yolks

85 g/3 oz caster sugar

300 ml/10 fl oz whole milk

250 g/9 oz plain chocolate

250 g/10 fl oz double cream

trellis cups

100 g/3^1/$_2$ oz plain chocolate

method

1 Beat the egg, egg yolks and caster sugar together in a mixing bowl until well combined. Heat the milk until it is almost boiling, then gradually pour it onto the eggs, whisking. Place the bowl over a saucepan of gently simmering water and cook, stirring constantly, until the custard mixture thickens sufficiently to thinly coat the back of a wooden spoon.

2 Break the chocolate into small pieces and add to the hot custard. Stir until the chocolate has melted. Cover with a sheet of dampened baking parchment and let it cool.

3 Whip the cream until just holding its shape, then fold into the cooled chocolate custard. Transfer to a freezerproof container and freeze for 1–2 hours until the mixture is frozen 2.5 cm/1 inch from the sides. Scrape the ice cream into a chilled bowl and beat again until smooth. Re-freeze until firm.

4 To make the trellis cups, invert a muffin pan and cover 6 alternate mounds with clingfilm. Melt the chocolate, place it in a paper pastry bag, and snip off the end.

5 Pipe a circle around the bottom of the mound, then pipe chocolate back and forth over it to form a double-thickness trellis. Pipe around the bottom again. Chill until set, then lift from the pan and remove the clingfilm. Serve the ice cream in the trellis cups.

marble cheesecake

ingredients

SERVES 10

base

225 g/8 oz toasted oat cereal

50 g/1³/₄ oz toasted
    hazelnuts, chopped

4 tbsp butter

25 g/1 oz plain chocolate

filling

350 g/12 oz full-fat soft cheese

100 g/3¹/₂ oz caster sugar

200 ml/7 fl oz thick yogurt

300 ml/10 fl oz double cream

1 envelope powdered gelatine

3 tbsp water

175 g/6 oz plain chocolate,
    melted

175 g/6 oz white chocolate,
    melted

method

1 Place the toasted oat cereal in a plastic bag and crush it roughly with a rolling pin. Pour the crushed cereal into a mixing bowl and stir in the toasted chopped hazelnuts.

2 Melt the butter and chocolate together over low heat and stir into the cereal mixture, stirring until well coated.

3 Using the bottom of a glass, press the mixture into the bottom and up the sides of a 20-cm/8-inch springform cake tin.

4 Beat the cheese and sugar together with a wooden spoon until smooth. Beat in the yogurt. Whip the cream until just holding its shape and fold into the mixture. Sprinkle the gelatine over the water in a heatproof bowl and let it go spongy. Place over a saucepan of hot water and stir until dissolved. Stir into the mixture.

5 Divide the mixture in half and beat the plain chocolate into one half and the white chocolate into the other half.

6 Place alternate spoonfuls of mixture on top of the cereal base. Swirl the filling together with the tip of a knife to give a marbled effect. Chill the cheesecake for at least 2 hours, until set, before serving.

chocolate marshmallow cake

ingredients

SERVES 6

6 tbsp unsalted butter

225 g/8 oz caster sugar

1/2 tsp vanilla essence

2 eggs, beaten lightly

85 g/3 oz plain chocolate,
    broken into pieces

150 ml/5 fl oz buttermilk

175 g/6 oz self-raising flour

1/2 tsp bicarbonate of soda

pinch of salt

marshmallow topping

175 g/6 oz white
    marshmallows

1 tbsp milk

2 egg whites

2 tbsp caster sugar

55 g/2 oz milk chocolate,
    grated, to decorate

method

1 Cream the butter, sugar and vanilla together in a bowl until pale and fluffy, then gradually beat in the eggs.

2 Melt the chocolate in a bowl over a saucepan of simmering water. Gradually stir in the buttermilk until well combined. Cool slightly.

3 Sift the flour, bicarbonate of soda and salt into a separate bowl. Add the chocolate and the flour mixtures alternately to the creamed mixture, a little at a time. Spoon the mixture into a 850-ml/1 1/2-pint ovenproof bowl greased with butter and smooth the surface. Bake in a preheated oven, 160°C/325°F, for 50 minutes until a skewer inserted into the centre of the cake comes out clean. Turn out onto a wire rack to cool.

4 Meanwhile, make the topping. Heat the marshmallows and milk very gently in a small saucepan until the marshmallows have melted. Remove from the heat and cool. Whisk the egg whites until soft peaks form, then add the sugar and continue whisking, until stiff peaks form. Fold into the cooled marshmallow mixture and set aside for 10 minutes.

5 When the cake is cool, cover the top and sides with the marshmallow topping. Top with grated milk chocolate.

double chocolate roulade

ingredients

SERVES 8

4 eggs, separated

115 g/4 oz golden caster sugar

115 g/4 oz plain chocolate, melted and cooled

1 tsp instant coffee granules, dissolved in 2 tbsp hot water, cooled

icing sugar, to decorate

cocoa powder, for dusting

fresh raspberries, to serve

filling

250 ml/9 fl oz whipping cream

140 g/5 oz white chocolate, broken into pieces

3 tbsp Tia Maria

method

1 Line a 23 x 33-cm/9 x 13-inch Swiss roll pan with nonstick baking parchment. Whisk the egg yolks and sugar in a bowl until pale and mousse-like. Fold in the chocolate, then the coffee. Place the egg whites in a clean bowl and whisk until stiff but not dry. Stir a little of the egg whites into the chocolate mixture, then fold in the remainder. Pour into the pan and bake in a preheated oven, 180°C/350°F, for 15–20 minutes, or until firm. Cover the tin with a damp tea towel and set aside for 8 hours, or overnight.

2 Meanwhile, make the filling. Heat the cream until almost boiling. Place the chocolate in a food processor and chop coarsely. With the motor running, pour the cream through the feed tube. Process until smooth. Stir in the Tia Maria. Transfer to a bowl and cool, then chill for 8 hours, or overnight.

3 To assemble the roulade, whip the chocolate cream until soft peaks form. Cut a sheet of waxed paper larger than the roulade, place on a work surface and sift icing sugar over it. Turn the roulade out onto the paper. Peel away the lining paper. Spread the chocolate cream over the roulade and roll up from the short side nearest to you. Transfer to a dish, seam-side down. Chill for 2 hours, then dust with cocoa. Serve with raspberries.

mocha layer cake

ingredients

SERVES 8

200 g/7 oz self-raising flour

1/4 tsp baking powder

4 tbsp cocoa powder

100 g/3 1/2 oz caster sugar

2 eggs

2 tbsp golden syrup

150 ml/5 fl oz corn oil

150 ml/5 fl oz milk

butter for greasing

filling

1 tsp instant coffee

1 tbsp boiling water

300 ml/10 fl oz double cream

2 tbsp icing sugar

to decorate

50 g/1 3/4 oz plain chocolate
    curls

chocolate caraque

icing sugar, for dusting

method

1 Sift the flour, baking powder and cocoa into a large bowl, then stir in the sugar. Make a well in the centre and stir in the eggs, syrup, corn oil and milk. Beat with a wooden spoon, gradually mixing in the dry ingredients to make a smooth batter. Divide the mixture between 3 lightly greased 18-cm/7-inch cake tins.

2 Bake in a preheated oven, 180°C/350°F, for 35–45 minutes, or until springy to the touch. Cool in the tins for 5 minutes, then turn out and cool completely on a wire rack.

3 To make the filling, dissolve the instant coffee in the boiling water and place in a large bowl with the cream and icing sugar. Whip until the cream is just holding its shape, then use half the cream to sandwich the 3 cakes together. Spread the remaining cream over the top and sides of the cake. Press the chocolate curls into the cream round the edge of the cake.

4 Transfer the cake to a serving plate. Lay the chocolate caraque over the top of the cake. Cut a few thin strips of baking parchment and place on top of the chocolate caraque. Dust lightly with icing sugar, then carefully remove the parchment. Serve.

chocolate passion cake

ingredients

SERVES 6

5 eggs

150 g/5^1/$_2$ oz caster sugar

150 g/5^1/$_2$ oz plain flour

40 g/1^1/$_2$ oz cocoa powder

175 g/6 oz carrots, peeled,
    finely grated, and
    squeezed until dry

50 g/1^3/$_4$ oz chopped walnuts

2 tbsp corn oil

butter, for greasing

350 g/12 oz medium-fat
    soft cheese

175 g/6 oz icing sugar

175 g/6 oz milk or plain
    chocolate, melted

method

1 Place the eggs and sugar in a large bowl set over a pan of gently simmering water and, using an electric whisk, whisk until the mixture is very thick and the whisk leaves a trail that lasts a few seconds when lifted.

2 Remove the bowl from the heat. Sift the flour and cocoa into the bowl and carefully fold in. Fold in the carrots, walnuts and corn oil until the cake batter is just blended.

3 Pour into a lightly greased and base-lined 20-cm/8-inch deep round cake tin and bake in a preheated oven, 190°C/375°F, for 45 minutes. Cool slightly in the tin, then turn out onto a wire rack to cool completely.

4 Beat the soft cheese and icing sugar together until blended, then beat in the melted chocolate. Split the cake in half and sandwich together again with half the chocolate mixture. Cover the top of the cake with the remainder of the chocolate mixture, swirling it with a knife. Chill in the refrigerator or serve immediately.

family chocolate cake

ingredients

SERVES 8

125 g/4^1/$_2$ oz soft margarine,
  plus extra for greasing
125 g/4^1/$_2$ oz caster sugar
2 eggs
1 tbsp golden syrup
125 g/4^1/$_2$ oz self-raising flour,
  sifted
2 tbsp cocoa powder, sifted
a little milk or white chocolate,
  melted (optional)

filling and topping

4 tbsp icing sugar, sifted
2 tbsp butter
100 g/3^1/$_2$ oz white or milk
  cooking chocolate

method

1 Place all of the ingredients for the cake in a large mixing bowl and beat with a wooden spoon or electric mixer to form a smooth mixture.

2 Divide the mixture between 2 lightly greased 18-cm/7-inch shallow cake tins and smooth the tops. Bake in a preheated oven, 190°C/ 375°F, for 20 minutes or until springy to the touch. Cool for a few minutes in the tins, then transfer to a wire rack to cool completely.

3 To make the filling, beat the sugar and butter together in a bowl until light and fluffy. Melt the white or milk cooking chocolate and beat half into the icing mixture. Use the filling to sandwich the 2 cakes together.

4 Spread the remaining melted cooking chocolate over the top of the cake. Pipe circles of contrasting milk or white chocolate and feather into the cooking chocolate with a cocktail stick, if desired. Allow the cake to set before serving.

cappuccino squares

ingredients

MAKES 15

225 g/8 oz self-raising flour

1 tsp baking powder

1 tsp cocoa powder,
    plus extra for dusting

225 g/8 oz butter, softened,
    plus extra for greasing

225 g/8 oz golden caster
    sugar

4 eggs, beaten

3 tbsp instant coffee powder,
    dissolved in 2 tbsp hot water

white chocolate frosting

115 g/4 oz white chocolate,
    broken into pieces

55 g/2 oz butter, softened

3 tbsp milk

175 g/6 oz icing sugar

method

1 Sift the flour, baking powder and cocoa into a bowl and add the butter, caster sugar, eggs and coffee. Beat well, by hand or with an electric whisk, until smooth, then spoon into a greased and base-lined shallow 28 x 18-cm/ 11 x 7-inch tin and smooth the top.

2 Bake in a preheated oven, 180°C/350°F, for 35–40 minutes, or until risen and firm, then turn out onto a wire rack, peel off the lining paper, and cool completely. To make the frosting, place the chocolate, butter and milk in a bowl set over a saucepan of simmering water and stir until the chocolate has melted.

3 Remove the bowl from the pan and sift in the icing sugar. Beat until smooth, then spread over the cake. Dust the top of the cake with sifted cocoa, then cut into rectangles or squares.

mocha brownies

ingredients

MAKES 16

55 g/2 oz butter, plus extra
for greasing

115 g/4 oz plain chocolate,
broken into pieces

175 g/6 oz brown sugar

2 eggs

1 tbsp instant coffee powder
dissolved in 1 tbsp hot
water, cooled

85 g/3 oz plain flour

1/2 tsp baking powder

55 g/2 oz roughly chopped
pecan nuts

method

1 Place the chocolate and butter in a heavy-based saucepan over low heat until melted. Stir and set aside to cool.

2 Place the sugar and eggs in a large bowl and cream together until light and fluffy. Fold in the chocolate mixture and cooled coffee and mix thoroughly. Sift in the flour and baking powder and lightly fold into the mixture, then carefully fold in the pecan nuts.

3 Pour the batter into a greased and base-lined 20-cm/8-inch square cake tin and bake in a preheated oven, 180°C/350°F, for 25–30 minutes, or until firm and a skewer inserted into the centre comes out clean.

4 Cool in the tin for a few minutes, then run a knife round the edge of the cake to loosen it. Turn the cake out onto a wire rack, peel off the lining paper, and cool completely. When cold, cut into squares.

caramel chocolate shortbread

ingredients

MAKES 24 PIECES

115 g/4 oz butter, plus extra
    for greasing
175 g/6 oz plain flour
55 g/2 oz golden caster sugar

filling and topping

175 g/6 oz butter
115 g/4 oz golden caster
    sugar
3 tbsp golden syrup
400 g/14 oz canned
    condensed milk
200 g/7 oz plain chocolate,
    broken into pieces

method

1 Place the butter, flour and sugar in a food processor and process until it begins to bind together. Press the mixture into a greased and base-lined 23-cm/9-inch shallow square cake tin and smooth the top. Bake in a preheated oven, 180°C/350°F, for 20–25 minutes, or until golden.

2 Meanwhile, make the filling. Place the butter, sugar, syrup and condensed milk in a saucepan and heat gently until the sugar has melted. Bring to the boil and simmer for 6–8 minutes, stirring constantly, until the mixture becomes very thick. Pour over the shortbread base and chill in the refrigerator until firm.

3 To make the topping, melt the chocolate and leave to cool, then spread over the caramel. Chill in the refrigerator until set. Cut the shortbread into 24 pieces with a sharp knife and serve.

chocolate butter biscuits

ingredients

MAKES ABOUT 18

100 g/3^1/$_2$ oz butter, softened,
 plus extra for greasing
100 g/3^1/$_2$ oz caster sugar
1 egg yolk
225 g/8 oz plain flour, sifted,
 plus extra for dusting
about 2 tbsp milk

icing

250 g/9 oz icing sugar, sifted
1 tbsp cocoa powder
about 3 tbsp orange juice

method

1 Put the butter and all but a tablespoon of the sugar into a large bowl and cream until pale and fluffy. Beat in the egg yolk, then add the flour and mix well. Stir in enough milk to form a smooth dough.

2 Roll out the dough on a lightly floured work surface. Cut out rounds using a 7.5-cm/3-inch biscuit cutter. Arrange the circles on 2 large, greased baking sheets, leaving enough space between them to allow them to spread during cooking. Sprinkle over the remaining sugar and bake in a preheated oven, 200°C/400°F, for 15 minutes, or until golden. Remove the biscuits from the oven, transfer to wire racks, and cool completely.

3 To make the icing, put the icing sugar and cocoa powder into a bowl. Stir in the orange juice gradually until enough has been added to make a thin icing. Put a teaspoonful of icing on each biscuit and let set before serving.

chocolate chip oaties

ingredients

MAKES ABOUT 20

115 g/4 oz butter, softened,
   plus extra for greasing

115 g/4 oz light brown sugar

1 egg

100 g/3$\frac{1}{2}$ oz rolled oats

1 tbsp milk

1 tsp vanilla essence

125 g/4$\frac{1}{2}$ oz plain flour

1 tbsp cocoa powder

$\frac{1}{2}$ tsp baking powder

175 g/6 oz plain chocolate,
   broken into pieces

175 g/6 oz milk chocolate,
   broken into pieces

method

1 Place the butter and sugar in a bowl and beat together until light and fluffy. Beat in the egg, then add the oats, milk and vanilla essence. Beat together until well blended. Sift the flour, cocoa powder and baking powder into the biscuit batter and stir. Stir in the chocolate pieces.

2 Place dessertspoonfuls of the biscuit batter on 2 greased baking sheets and flatten slightly with a fork. Bake in a preheated oven, 180°C/350°F, for 15 minutes, or until slightly risen and firm. Let cool on the baking sheets for 2 minutes, then transfer to wire racks to cool completely.

mocha walnut biscuits

ingredients

MAKES ABOUT 16

115 g/4 oz butter, softened,
    plus extra for greasing

115 g/4 oz light brown sugar

85 g/3 oz golden granulated
    sugar

1 tsp vanilla essence

1 tbsp instant coffee
    granules, dissolved in
    1 tbsp hot water

1 egg

175 g/6 oz plain flour

$1/2$ tsp baking powder

$1/4$ tsp bicarbonate of soda

55 g/2 oz milk chocolate
    chips

55 g/2 oz shelled walnuts,
    roughly chopped

method

1 Place the butter, brown sugar and granulated sugar in a large mixing bowl and beat together thoroughly until light and fluffy. Place the vanilla essence, coffee and egg in a separate bowl and whisk together.

2 Gradually add the coffee mixture to the butter and sugar, beating until fluffy. Sift the flour, baking powder and bicarbonate of soda into the biscuit batter and fold in carefully. Fold in the chocolate chips and walnuts.

3 Place dessertspoonfuls of the biscuit batter onto 2 greased baking sheets, allowing room for the biscuits to spread. Bake in a preheated oven, 180°C/350°F, for 10–15 minutes, or until crisp on the outside but still soft inside. Cool on the baking sheets for 2 minutes, then transfer to wire racks to cool completely.

ladies kisses

ingredients

MAKES 20

140 g/5 oz unsalted butter

115 g/4 oz caster sugar

1 egg yolk

115 g/4 oz ground almonds

175 g/6 oz plain flour

55 g/2 oz plain chocolate,
    broken into pieces

2 tbsp icing sugar

2 tbsp cocoa powder

method

1 Beat the butter and sugar together in a bowl until pale and fluffy. Beat in the egg yolk, then beat in the almonds and flour. Continue beating until well mixed. Shape the dough into a ball, wrap in clingfilm and chill in the refrigerator for 1^1/$_2$–2 hours.

2 Unwrap the dough, break off walnut-size pieces, and roll them into balls between the palms of your hands. Place the dough balls on 3 baking sheets lined with baking parchment, allowing room for expansion during cooking. Bake in a preheated oven, 160°C/325°F, for 20–25 minutes, or until golden brown. Carefully transfer the biscuits, still on the baking parchment, to wire racks to cool.

3 Place the plain chocolate in a small heatproof bowl and set over a saucepan of barely simmering water, stirring constantly, until melted. Remove from the heat.

4 Remove the biscuits from the baking parchment, and spread the melted chocolate over the bases. Sandwich them together in pairs and return to the wire racks to cool. Dust with a mixture of icing sugar and cocoa powder and serve.

chocolate viennese fingers

ingredients

MAKES ABOUT 30

115 g/4 oz butter, softened,
    plus extra for greasing
55 g/2 oz golden icing sugar,
    sifted
125 g/4^1/$_2$ oz plain flour
1 tbsp cocoa powder
100 g/3^1/$_2$ oz plain chocolate,
    melted and cooled

method

1 Beat the butter and sugar together until light and fluffy. Sift the flour and cocoa powder into the bowl and work the mixture until it is a smooth, piping consistency.

2 Spoon into a large piping bag fitted with a 2.5-cm/1-inch fluted tip. Pipe 6-cm/2^1/$_2$-inch lengths of the mixture onto 2 greased baking sheets, allowing room for expansion during cooking. Bake in a preheated oven, 180°C/350°F, for 15 minutes, or until firm.

3 Cool on the baking sheets for 2 minutes, then transfer to a wire rack to cool completely. Dip the ends of the biscuits into the melted chocolate and allow to set before serving.

easy chocolate fudge

ingredients

MAKES 25 PIECES

75 g/2³/4 oz unsalted butter,
    cut into even-size pieces,
    plus extra for greasing
500 g/1 lb 2 oz plain
    chocolate
400 g/14 oz canned sweetened
    condensed milk
¹/2 tsp vanilla essence

method

1 Lightly grease a 20-cm/8-inch square cake tin with butter. Break the chocolate into small pieces and place in a large, heavy-based saucepan with the butter and condensed milk.

2 Heat gently, stirring constantly, until the chocolate and butter melt and the mixture is smooth. Do not let boil. Remove from the heat. Beat in the vanilla essence, then beat the mixture for a few minutes until thickened. Pour it into the tin and level the top.

3 Chill the mixture in the refrigerator for 1 hour, or until firm. Tip the fudge out onto a cutting board and cut into squares to serve.

This edition published by Parragon in 2008

Parragon
Queen Street House
4 Queen Street
Bath BA1 1HE, UK

Copyright © Parragon Books Ltd 2007

ISBN 978-1-4075-3088-8

All rights reserved. No part of this publication may be reproduced, stored in a retrieval system or transmitted in any form or by any means, electronic, mechanical, photocopying, recording or otherwise, without the prior permission of the copyright holder.

Printed in China

Notes for the reader
• This book uses both metric and imperial measurements. Follow the same units of measurement throughout; do not mix metric and imperial. All spoon measurements are level: teaspoons are assumed to be 5 ml, and tablespoons are assumed to be 15 ml. Unless otherwise stated, milk is assumed to be full fat, eggs and individual vegetables are medium, and pepper is freshly ground black pepper.
• The times given are an approximate guide only. Preparation times differ according to the techniques used by different people and the cooking times may also vary from those given. Optional ingredients, variations or serving suggestions have not been included in the calculations.
• Recipes using raw or very lightly cooked eggs should be avoided by infants, the elderly, pregnant women, convalescents and anyone suffering from an illness. Pregnant and breastfeeding women are advised to avoid eating peanuts and peanut products. Sufferers from nut allergies should be aware that some of the ready-made ingredients used in the recipes in this book may contain nuts. Always check the packaging before use.